A TEEN'S GAME PLAN FOR LIFE

LOU HOLTZ

A TEEN'S GAME PLAN FOR LIFE

LOU HOLTZ

SORIN BOOKS  Notre Dame, Indiana

www.sorinbooks.com

ISBN-10 1-933495-09-X   ISBN-13 978-1-933495-09-5

Project Editor: Michael Amodei

Cover and text design by Andy Wagoner

Photography Credits:
© Icon SMI/Corbis: p. 34
Vince Wehby: p. 40
© Smirnov Vladimir/ITAR-TASS/Corbis: p. 44
© Jan Butchofsky-Houser/Corbis: p. 61
© Associated Press/AP: p. 83, 92
© ESPN: p. 108, 122

Printed and bound in the United States of America.

Library of Congress Cataloging-in-Publication Data is available.

CONTENTS

A LETTER TO ALL TEENS

FROM LOU HOLTZ

Because of today's social climate,
your ability to know how to make
good decisions becomes
more important than ever before.

TO MY TEENAGE FRIENDS,

You have more choices and decisions before you than any previous generation.

Because of the increase in the number of families with both parents working, and the increase in the number of single parent families, you are being asked, on your own, to make important decisions that have adult consequences earlier than any previous generation. I imagine a number of you already perform adult functions, like providing care, supervising, and cooking for a younger sibling. You are to be commended.

So often the good achievements of young people go unnoticed while bad actions like school shootings, drug overdoses, or a teenage killing over a pair of sneakers make the headlines today.

Why would a teenager take such extreme actions that tarnish the reputation of an entire generation, you may ask? Some of these incidents may involve drug use, or a lack of respect brought on by low self-esteem. Some actions are beyond comprehension.

However, we do know that when a young person performs actions such as these, they are stealing future opportunities and chances from themselves.

Because of today's social climate, your ability to know how to make good decisions becomes more important than ever before.

The nature of making good decisions and leading successful lives remains the same as when your parents and grandparents were your age. How to make those decisions and understand some of the important things of life is what I hope to pass on to you.

I will share some simple and easy-to-apply rules for success that I have used myself. Believe it or not, I was once a teenager, too. In fact, I wasn't a good student and I wasn't a good athlete. My gift was common sense, something I have been fortunate enough to have possessed my whole life.

I'm going to share with you a game plan for life that I hope will help you to understand what is important and how you can make good decisions in the future.

I believe this is a formula for success that you can use from this day forward.

My prayers are with you as you try to be all that God intends for you.

THE PLAYBOOK

*I know what it's like to be up one day
and down the other.*

I've been there.

We all have.

PLAY 1
CHOOSE YOUR ATTITUDE

God gave you power to love and think, to create and imagine, and to plan. But the greatest power you have is the power to choose.

You're going to choose whether you act or procrastinate, whether you believe or doubt.

You are also going to choose whether or not you are going to be happy or sad, succeed or fail.

You're going to choose your attitude.

Those are choices!

One year Notre Dame was scheduled to play on New Year's Day against the University of Florida in the Sugar Bowl. I felt Notre Dame would play very well. I sent our football team home for two days at Christmas to spend time with their families. I've always believed this is important. That year my wife and children and I gathered in Orlando.

We have four children, and they're all girls but two, and I'm very proud of them. I'm never happier than when I'm with my children. We were sitting in a restaurant and the waiter recognized me and came over. He said, "You're Lou Holtz, the coach of Notre Dame, aren't you?"

I said, "Yes, sir," and I took out my pen because I thought he wanted my autograph.

He waved me off and said, "I've got a question, Coach. What's the difference between Notre Dame and Cheerios?"

I said, "Gee, I don't know."

He said, "Cheerios belong in a bowl, and Notre Dame doesn't."

This is a true story. Well, my attitude changed.

I looked at him and said, "Let me ask you a question. What's the difference between Lou Holtz and a golf pro?"

He shook his head like he didn't know.

I said, "A golf pro gives tips."

The point is I could have let what one individual said put me in a bad mood and ruin an evening with the people I love the most. Or I could make a joke about it and move on.

The talent you have determines what God gave you the ability to do. It's your attitude that determines how well you accomplish things you want to do.

I can't run the 100 in 10.5 seconds. I don't have that talent.

But consider someone who is capable of running it in 10.5. He may not be motivated to run, so he doesn't even go out for track. Or another guy capable of running a 10.5 may come out for track, but he doesn't really push himself and he runs an 11.3. Attitude will determine a lot of things.

onsider Jerome Bettis. Number 36 for the Pittsburgh Steelers. He played for me at the University of Notre Dame. After Notre Dame he went to the then Los Angeles Rams in the NFL and became the league's rookie of the year.

His second year in the pros Jerome wasn't very good. The third year everybody said he was washed up.

I watched the Rams play on TV, and Jerome didn't play very well. I called him on the phone, and I said, "Jerome, this is Coach Holtz. I watched the Rams play, and there's some guy impersonating you, wearing your jersey and your number, and giving you a bad name. You gotta put a stop to it."

I hung up the phone.

As soon as the season was over Jerome Bettis showed up at my office. He said, "Coach, when I left Notre Dame I had a wonderful attitude. I went to the pros, and I let my attitude go down. I'm coming back to Notre Dame. And I'm going to spend the next four months here getting my attitude right." And that's what he did. He spent the summer at Notre Dame working out and rededicating himself to being the best football player he could be.

In that off-season Jerome was traded to the Pittsburgh Steelers. He became the famous "Bus," the league leader in rushing and eventually only the fourteenth player to rush for over 10,000 yards in a career. The Steelers did not get the same Jerome Bettis who played the year before with the Rams.

Same talent. Different attitude. Different results.

There was another young man at Notre Dame named Mike Brennan. Mike Brennan was from Baltimore. He walked on to the team without a scholarship. And he was the slowest player I've ever seen in my life, bar none.

If we had run Mike Brennan on a sweep, we would have been called for a delay of game penalty. I mean this guy was slow.

The players nicknamed him "Turtle." I didn't like that. I thought that was very disparaging to the turtle. But that's what the players called him. If you were to come back to Notre Dame today and say, "Hey, who's the 'Turtle'?" everybody would say, "Mike Brennan."

I said this guy would never play for us.

But I underestimated Mike. What he lacked in speed he made up in attitude. Mike Brennan made up his mind that he was going to play. And when we beat Miami 31–30, the number one ranked team at the time, who started for Notre Dame? Mike Brennan. And who played four years in the NFL? That same Mike Brennan.

It's attitude. And a positive attitude is a choice you make.

The problem is, that it's easy to adopt the attitude of losers.

And the only people in this world who are ever going to try to pull you down are those who are down.

The ones who are going to lift you up are the ones who believe in themselves and what they are doing.

When I think of someone who believed in himself, I think of a football player from Troy, Ohio, named Ryan Brewer. Ryan received quite a few honors in high school.

Shortly after being named head coach at South Carolina, I got a personal call from Ryan. He told me that he had been a fan of mine since seventh grade and he wanted to come to South Carolina to play football for me. When I learned that Ryan was named "Mr. Football" in Ohio I told him that we would recruit him. Right over the phone Ryan said, "Then I commit to the University of South Carolina."

When I found out that Ryan didn't have any other scholarship offers and realized we hadn't seen any film of him playing, I started getting a little nervous. But we had given him our word and we certainly would honor it.

Ryan arrived on campus. He was 5'8" and 205 pounds. Like Mike Brennan, he didn't possess exceptional quickness and speed.

But he also had a marvelous attitude.

His work habits were excellent, and he was an outstanding competitor. He

immediately earned the respect of his teammates. Ryan lettered for us playing tailback
as a freshman even though he didn't do anything outstanding. But keep in mind that
nobody on our 1999 football team did.

In the winter after that season Ryan
worked so hard and was so positive that we
felt we just had to find a place for him on the
field. We moved Ryan to wide receiver and
he performed very, very well.

Our second season, 2000, was much better. We were invited to play Ohio State in the
January 1 Outback Bowl. As we got ready
for that game, we had to suspend our start-
ing tailback who had gained almost 1,100
yards. We had no choice but to return Ryan
Brewer to tailback.

Ryan's performance was outstanding.
He rushed for over 100 yards, caught passes
for over 100 yards, and scored three touch-
downs. He was the most valuable player in
our 24–7 victory, enabling us to finish ranked
nineteenth in the country that year after not
winning any games the year before.

I ask you, how was this player different from the one whom no one thought deserved a scholarship?

It was Ryan's attitude that made all the difference.

I cannot emphasize enough the importance of having a good attitude. When you get up in the morning, the attitude you choose is the most critical thing that you do.

PLAY 2
MAKE SACRIFICES

If you're going to be successful, the second thing you need to understand is that you will have to make sacrifices.

Sometimes we make fun of people who make sacrifices. I ran into a young lady on the elevator, and she looked like she was going jogging. I asked her how far she was going to run. She said, "Six miles."

I told her, "I don't even drive that far."

She looked at me and said, "So you jog?"

I said, "Oh, no. I want to be sick when I die."

can kid around about being committed to something, but in fact I truly admire people who are willing to make whatever sacrifices it takes to be successful.

I happen to be where I am today because of the sacrifices made by others for me. When I was in high school all I ever wanted out of life was a job in the mill, five dollars in my pocket, and a girl on my arm. I couldn't have imagined any more out of life because I didn't have much to begin with.

But my high school coach thought differently and told my parents, "Lou Holtz ought to go to college and be a football coach."

I didn't want to go to college. But my parents wanted me to go to college. So we compromised and I went to college. That was a typical compromise for us in our family. But in order for me to go to college, my mother had to go to work as a nurse's aide on the night shift—from eleven at night until seven in the morning. She made thirty-five dollars a week.

I went to college because of the sacrifices that my mother made.

She showed me that you will never succeed unless you are willing to make a sacrifice both for yourself and others.

I've gone into losing situations several times as a coach. When I became head coach at Notre Dame, it had just lost the last game of its season to Miami, 58–7. Morale wasn't very high. I walked into the staff room with my new assistant coaches when we were first hired and said, "You know we're going to have to win early because Notre Dame isn't real patient."

That meant hard work and sacrifice. But we had problems right away. All the players complained because they had to lift weights, they had to work out, and they had to practice hard. We were determined not to accept anything less, but still they complained.

This is what happens when you are losing. You're going to complain about how much work you have. You're going to find a hundred things to complain about on a continuous basis.

So think before you complain, especially about things that require some sacrifice. Complaining is the sign of a loser.

Related to sacrifice is self-discipline. Discipline is not what you do to somebody. Discipline is what you do *for* somebody.

As a coach, I don't really discipline people. "Well," you say, "you sent the leading ground gainer and the leading receiver home before the 1988 Notre Dame-Southern Cal game because they were late to a team meal." This was a battle between two teams ranked number one and two in the country.

That's true. But it wasn't my choice. It was the players' choice. All I did was enforce their decision. They had been late before and I told them, "If you do this one more time— your fault, my fault, bus driver's fault, heart attack, I don't care—you're choosing not to play in the game."

They chose to violate the rules. I didn't discipline them. I enforced their decision. Abiding by the rules of those in authority in your lives—your parents, teachers, coaches —requires self-discipline.

The self-discipline of our players was a big reason the University of South Carolina was successful in the 2001 Outback Bowl.

We knew we would have a tremendous challenge playing Ohio State. We also were aware of the fact that South Carolina had only won one bowl game in its entire history.

We told our players that they shouldn't be too excited. Getting to the bowl game was the easy part. Winning the bowl game is a much more difficult thing to do, particularly since

South Carolina had not enjoyed a great deal of success in bowl games in the past.

We asked our players to do two things. The first was to trust the coaches and the system, due to the fact that I and many of our coaches had been to several bowl games with other universities. The players realized that we had an awful lot of experience and that they had none, so they were willing to give us that trust.

The second thing we asked them to do was to work very hard. If we were going to win, they would have to make sacrifices. They would have to continue to lift weights, practice, and at the same time keep up with their academics. In addition to that, they would only be able to go home for two days at Christmas.

In other words, winning the bowl game was going to take sacrifice and self-discipline.

I told them we would make some mistakes in the bowl game and that I would certainly forgive any mistake they made whether it was a fumble, an interception, a missed block, or a missed tackle. But the one mistake I would never forgive, nor would they forgive, was failing to prepare properly. I must say that our football team prepared as hard and as valiantly as any I've been associated with.

You may not remember this game between South Carolina and Ohio State. But let me tell you that the first half we dominated play—four times we were inside the Ohio State twenty yard line. But we made every mistake known to mankind inside the twenty. We missed field goals, we fumbled, and we threw an interception right before the half. The list goes on and on and we went into the locker room with only a three-point lead.

Nevertheless, the players never let losing enter their minds. They trusted each other. They trusted the coaches. And most of all they trusted themselves.

We came out in the second half and again completely dominated the game. But this time we made fewer mistakes against an excellent Ohio State team and ultimately won 24–7.

That's what results from sacrifice and self-discipline.

Remember, every decision you make sets the stage for different results.

When you choose not to study, you're going to get poor grades. When you choose not to work out hard, you're choosing not to win.

Practice to the very best of your ability to be ready to do your very best. That's what I mean by sacrifice and self-discipline.

In the late 1960s, I coached with a man named Woody Hayes at Ohio State. In case you haven't heard, Woody Hayes was one of the greatest coaches of all time. The last time Ohio State won a national championship, I happened to be on Coach Hayes' staff. When we played Purdue that year it was number one in the country. We beat them. I was really excited because I had all my relatives at the game. All my high school friends and fraternity buddies were there as well. We planned to party after that game.

But Coach Hayes had other ideas. He told all of the assistants to meet in the staff room at seven o'clock on Saturday night after the game.

He wanted to begin preparations for the next opponent, and I just wanted to party. But we prepared for the next opponent and went on to win. That year we won the national championship because Woody Hayes had standards. He demanded sacrifice and self-discipline from those around him.

You're going to have to do the same in whatever you choose to do.

PLAY 3

GET RID OF EXCUSES

When I went to Notre Dame in 1986, the team had come off a losing season.

When I introduced myself to the football team I told them, "We're not going to win because I'm here any more than someone can fix a flat tire by changing the driver. If we're going to be successful, we have to get rid of all the excuses for why we can't win."

It was one of a number of things we were going to have to change.

We played the University of Michigan in the opening game of my first season. They were number two in the country and had a great quarterback named Jim Harbaugh. Although we outplayed Michigan —we played a superb game—we unfortunately made a few mistakes. We lost a heartbreaker 24–23.

When you went into our locker room after the game, you could see we still had a lot of work to do. Despite making the kind of progress that allowed us to play the number two team in the nation so well, players were blaming other players for the loss. Players were pointing fingers.

"He fumbled."

"He threw an interception."

"He dropped a pass."

"He missed a field goal."

"The official made a bad call."

"Coach Holtz made a lot of bad decisions."

In other words, it was everybody else's fault. The players were willing to use someone else's mistake as an excuse for not succeeding.

You have to get rid of all the excuses for why you can't do something.

Like the players after the Michigan game, you can find lots of reasons why you can't do something. "This is wrong. That's wrong. This is against me."

As long as you can find excuses, you don't have a chance.

The second game was against Michigan State at East Lansing. They had a fine football team, and the game was on national television. Three minutes to go, and we were getting beat 20–15. We had the ball inside their twenty-five yard line.

All we had to do was score a touchdown, and we would win.

I called a time out. I called the team over and said, "Men, we're going to throw a pass. We're going to run Right 324 SXB pass."

Now I understand that play means absolutely nothing to you. What I didn't realize at the time was that it didn't mean much to our quarterback either. He threw an interception, and we ended up losing the football game.

The whole year went along that way. We lost heartbreaker after heartbreaker and it was always somebody else's fault.

In our very last game in my first year at Notre Dame, we played our archrival Southern Cal. There were 90,000 hostile fans at the Los Angeles Memorial Coliseum for the game. USC had an excellent football team and a great quarterback by the name of Rodney Peete. We were a decided underdog in the football game.

With eleven minutes to go in the game, we were getting beat 30–20. Southern Cal had a fourth down and five yards to go at midfield and went into punt formation. The best chance we had to win the game was to throw on a punt rush and block the punt. We did put on the punt rush. We did not block the punt.

But we did succeed in roughing the punter and getting a penalty which gave the ball and a first down to Southern Cal.

Now the young man guilty of roughing the punter happened to be my wife's son. After the game the reporters said to me, "What'd you think when your son roughed the punter?" I said, "Now I can understand how certain species of animals devour their young."

Southern Cal went on to score as a result of this play and made it 37–20 with nine minutes to go in the game.

But when our football team gathered together to receive the next kickoff there was something different about them. I don't know if they were embarrassed over the stupid penalty or tired of losing, but they stopped making excuses and made a commitment to each other.

They were going to run the kickoff back.

They said, "You get your guy, and I'll get my guy." We didn't run it all the way back, but we ran it back far enough to set up a touchdown.

Then our defense went out and said "We're going to stop them." And that was amazing. They had struggled all year. But they came together in the last minutes of the last game of the season and stopped Southern Cal. And in those last nine minutes we scored eighteen points and won the game 38–37.

From that time on, we won over eighty percent of our football games at Notre Dame during the next ten years. Not because of something I did. But because a group of people learned that you can only be successful when you get rid of all the excuses.

EVERYBODY is going to have problems.

EVERYBODY is going to get knocked down.

EVERYBODY is going to have difficulty.

The question is, "Are you going to stay down, or are you going to get up?" Success is getting up after you get knocked down.

I grew up near the Ohio River. As teenagers we used to go swimming in the Ohio where it crossed into Chester, West Virginia.

We were swimming one day, and someone got the bright idea that we ought to swim across the river, a distance of about one mile. And whoever finished last would walk back across the bridge, get the car, drive back, and pick up the rest of us.

Just when we were about to start, my best friend Nevitt Stockdale said, "I'm not going."

I said, "What do you mean, you're not going?"

He said, "I can't swim that far."

"Oh, Nevitt, you can make it. And if you can't make it, I'll save you," I encouraged him.

Now it was important to me that Nevitt try to swim because he was the only one I was sure I could beat.

"You'd do that for me?" Nevit questioned.

I said, "You've got my word."

We started out. We got a quarter of the way across that river, and Nevitt was doing super.

We got halfway across the river, and Nevitt was doing great.

We got three-quarters of the way across the river, and Nevitt started to struggle. As he predicted and in spite of doing fine until then, he said he didn't think he could make it all the way across.

He called on me to save him as I had promised. And I did the same thing that you might have done if you were in my situation. I tried to pretend that I couldn't hear him calling to me.

Nevitt was my best friend as long as my feet could touch ground. But in the water I was worried first about Lou Holtz.

Everyone else had already finished and there was just Nevitt and me three-quarters of the way across that river. Nevitt pleaded for help, but no one came to his aid. Finally he did the only thing he could logically do to save his life: he turned around and swam back.

He ended up swimming a mile and a half because deep down inside he didn't believe that he could swim a mile across the river. He didn't believe strongly enough in himself. He had an excuse not to succeed.

PLAY 4

UNDERSTAND WHAT YOU'RE TRYING TO DO

Another thing that is important is understanding what it is you are trying to do.

What about you?

Are you trying to be the most popular person at school?

Are you trying to help other people?

Are you trying to get an education or just trying to skate through?

Just ask yourself, "What am I trying to do?" It's important you know the answer to that question.

Notre Dame is a special university. Why? It understands what it is trying to do. Education is its first priority. Always. In every circumstance.

The purpose of the University is to educate all its students. Period. It has a faculty because it has students. It has coaches because it has athletes.

Every decision Notre Dame makes is centered on how it can *best* educate these students. That's how its decisions are always made. Notre Dame understands what it has to do.

Life is not all that complicated. Just ask yourself, "What am I trying to do?"

You want to open up a business?

Let me tell you about business. It's simple.

All you're trying to do in business is to help people get what they need and want. And it's about determining what they want and need.

But peoples' needs and wants change.

And life changes.

And your life is going to change.

So don't fight change.

In 1963, I got a job selling cemetery plots. When I got that job my wife told me, "You won't sell anything." Well, she understood me better than I understood myself. I didn't sell many cemetery plots and ended up selling our car, our stereo, and our television just to pay bills. I learned that I wasn't an effective salesman. It wasn't what I wanted to do.

In the 1870s some business people determined that other business people could benefit from the typewriter. So in 1878 they brought the typewriter to market. It was a success, but soon there was a serious problem. People learned to type so well and so fast that the keys stuck. So they said, "How can we keep the keys from sticking?"

Do you know what they decided to do?

They decided to slow down the typists. They rearranged the letters on the keypad putting the most used letters in the hardest to reach spots. They put an "e" up here, an "o" over there, and stuck a "c" way down in the corner. They figured nobody would be able to type very fast because they would have to hunt for the letters.

They met the need for change. And it worked. Or at least it worked long enough for better machines to be built.

Now what about today? There is no way you can stick any key on today's keyboards no matter how fast you type. But if you tried to change the order of the letters now everybody would get mad. They've learned the current system and don't want to change, even if a different arrangement of letters would work better. That's true. It's been tried. And the rearranged keyboard hasn't caught on.

Nobody wants change.

If you go out for a sport or decide to take part in an extracurricular activity like a language club, then stay with it for the entire season or year. My wife and I insisted on this with our kids. We expected them to keep their commitment whether or not they liked the coach, whether or not they won or lost, whether they played or sat on the bench. Quitting would be the easy way out.

But change is good if you understand what you're trying to do. So if you understand that something is not for you after honoring your initial commitment, then make that decision thoughtfully and move on to something else. I've always believed that if you drop one activity you should replace it with another, with something you find worthwhile. Use the newfound time to improve yourself.

Always stop and ask yourself, "What is the right thing to do?" and ask, "What am I trying to do?"

PLAY 5

DREAM BIG DREAMS

If there's one thing in this world that's been exciting for me, it's been dreaming big dreams and then having them come true.

One dream I had early in my coaching career was to coach at Notre Dame. So when I took the head football coach's job at the University of Minnesota, I negotiated my dream into my contract there. If the Notre Dame job were offered to me, I could take it.

Dreams make things happen.

When you find out about anybody who's ever been successful, you find out that they've had dreams.

I was with Michael Jordan recently, and he told me about his dream to play basketball for the University of North Carolina. He had dreams about what he wanted to do, and he made his dreams happen. He played for North Carolina and was on a national championship team there.

I started naming my dreams when I was twenty-eight. And that's when I really started acting on my dreams. Before that I just sort of went along.

This was in 1966 when I took a job at the University of South Carolina as an assistant football coach under a head coach by the name of Marvin Bass. My wife was eight months pregnant with our third child Kevin. I was there only about a month when I picked up the paper and read the headline "Marvin Bass Resigns." I said to my wife, "I wonder if he's related to my coach."

Well, obviously they were one and the same and the next thing you know I was unemployed. My wife had to go to work, and I stayed home. And I got this book. It said that if you're bored with life, if you don't have a burning desire for anything, you should name your dreams and write them down. I started really thinking about my life. What were the things I wanted to do? What did I want to accomplish?

So I broke my dreams down to five categories.

- Things I wanted to do religiously and spiritually.

- Things I wanted to do as a husband and father.

- Things I wanted to accomplish professionally.

- Things I wanted to accomplish financially.

- Things I wanted to do for excitement.

Then I started listing all my dreams in each of these categories. For example:

- I wanted to parachute out of an airplane.

- And I wanted to land on an aircraft carrier.

- And go in a submarine.

- Be on *The Tonight Show*.

- I wanted to go white-water rafting in Hell's Canyon on the Snake River.

- I wanted to go to the White House for dinner.

- I wanted to see the pope.

- I wanted to go to the Holy Land.

- I wanted to go on an African safari.

- I wanted to go to Pamplona and run with the bulls (but with a person slower than I).

I wrote down all 107 of them. My wife came home and I said to her, "Here's one hundred and seven of my dreams. We're going to do them all."

She looked at them and said, "Gee, that's great. Why don't you go ahead and get a job?"

So we made it 108.

We have done 101 of my dreams so far. I know what it's like to come out of an airplane at 10,000 feet. Free-fall 5,000 feet in forty-five seconds. Pull the chute and fall the other 5,000 feet in seven and a half minutes. I'm not ever going to do it again. But every time I go up in an airplane and we get to 10,000 feet, I think of the three guys who pushed me out when I changed my mind and decided that jumping might not be such a good idea.

I know what it's like to be on *The Tonight Show*.

I know what it's like to go white-water rafting. When I saw it on TV, it looked like fun. So I got my four children, their spouses, my wife, and my seventy-six-year-old mother-in-law. I hired a professional guide. We went to Hell's Canyon. Four days, three nights.

I put on my vest, and we got in that raft. I'm not in there ten minutes when a guide says, "Coach, get ready, we're going through Big Chain." I said, "What's that?" He said that's a "class five" rapids. I didn't even

know they were classified. He says that's the most dangerous you can go through.

I said, "Give me an example of a 'class six' rapids."

He answered, "Niagara Falls."

Boy, I stuck my thumb down in that little gunwale rope you hold on to for stability. When we hit that rapids, my feet came up over my head and I came out of that raft three seconds before my right thumb.

I broke my right thumb in four places.

But I didn't know that right away because I had another, more immediate, problem. I came up underneath the raft. They didn't teach me to moonwalk way underneath the raft. So I went back down thinking the raft wouldn't continue, but I was still going at the same rate of speed—under the raft.

The second time I came up underneath the raft I realized that winning the national championship wasn't that important. There was only one thought on my mind—it was the word WIN, or "What's Important Now." And if anything was important now, it was to get out from underneath the raft. With this realization I finally got my head above water and kept it there.

It's great to have big dreams. But the way to make your dreams come true is through a series of smaller daily choices. This is where the WIN formula can help.

You want to graduate tops in your class, or be an All-American? Then ask yourself twenty-five times a day, "What's important now?"

You wake up in the morning—"What's important now?" Get out of bed.

You're out of bed—"What's important now?" Eat breakfast. You need your strength.

"What's important now?" Go to class.

"What's important now?" Sit in the front row. Be prepared.

It's time to practice. "What's important now?" Use the weight room. It's there to help you get stronger. You don't use it because someone's looking, but because you know you've got to get stronger.

When you're out Saturday night and there's opportunities for alcohol, or sex, or drugs? "What's important now?" If your dream is to be outstanding in whatever field

you've chosen, then "what's important now"
is to avoid these situations.

WIN
WHAT'S **I**MPORTANT **N**OW

There is no way in the world you can enjoy success if you don't have ambitions, and if you don't have dreams. You have to do more, though, than name your dreams. You have to have high expectations for yourself. You have to act on them or your dreams will never become a reality.

I am a great believer that dreams do come true and miracles do happen, but only if you begin to expect more of yourself. A wise person once said, "If you keep doing what you have always been doing, you will keep getting the same results." Your results will not change until you change your standards or expectations.

At one time while I was at the University of Notre Dame, we had fifty-five former players in the NFL at the same time. The next highest was Penn State with thirty-eight. These were all young men who had dreams and acted on them. I honestly believe that many players from our team at the University of South Carolina will reach the NFL because this is their dream. But while they will continue to dream, they will also continue to raise their level of expectations and the level

of standards for themselves in every area of their lives—in their personal conduct, their academic progress, as well as in their athletic endeavors.

Did you know there is a very fine line between the physical characteristics of a winning team and a losing team? When you analyze it, the height, weight, and speed of a winning team and a losing team will usually be very, very close. I know this personally because we have done this analysis since we have been at the University of South Carolina.

One year, the difference between the total height of our whole team and the total height of the team that won the conference was less than 1/8 of an inch. We also weighed a total of one pound more than the conference champion. I couldn't verify the differences in team speed, but I don't think there was much difference in speed between us either.

Then what accounts for a team winning championships and another being an also-ran?

In our case, once we started dreaming bigger and believing we could achieve our dreams—because we were already so much like teams that were champions—our football team changed and became successful, too.

The last thing I have to tell you about dreams involved our football team at Notre Dame. We were going to open the season against the University of Michigan.

As practices began that summer our players had great excitement and looked forward to beating Michigan. But as summer two-a-days wore on they seemed not to care so much about Michigan anymore. Why? They were tired, they were uncomfortable, and they just went through the bare minimal effort at practices.

That's the thing with dreams. At first we get all excited. And then we have a little bit of adversity, and we lose sight of our dreams. That's natural. But it takes an unnatural person to continue to believe that dream and to follow it.

I walked out about the tenth day of practice before the Michigan game and I called the team together. "I know you're tired," I told them. "So I called Bo Schembechler." (I didn't really call Bo, the Michigan coach, but I told them I did.)

I told them that the conversation between Bo and me went this way:

"Bo, are your Michigan players tired?"

"Yeah, they're tired."

"Bo, we're tired too. I tell you what, you give the Michigan players a day off, and I'm going to give the Notre Dame players a day off."

Boy, you never saw such excitement when my players heard this. They started high fivin' each other, cheering wildly.

I interrupted them. "Bo said 'no.'"

They looked at me in disbelief. I repeated, "Bo said 'no.' Bo said he didn't care how tired you were. He was going to practice." I told them, "I don't want to practice you, but if we're going to beat Michigan, we've got to practice."

We had a great practice. Because they remembered their dream.

It worked so well that I tried it again before the next practice. I told them that I just spoke with Bo on the telephone. They looked at me real funny and asked what happened.

I told them I asked Bo if his players were sore, and that Bo admitted that his players were indeed sore.

I told them I offered, "Bo, you practice your team in shorts, and I'll practice my team in shorts.

"Men, you won't believe this. Bo said 'no.' Said he's going to scrimmage. I don't want to scrimmage, but if we're going to beat Michigan we've got to scrimmage. Don't get mad at me, but you remember this when you see Bo on September 12. He's the guy doing this to you."

We had a great scrimmage. I did the same thing for three more days. I walked out the sixth day and before I could say anything one of our players said, "I called Bo today."

I asked him what Bo said.

"Bo said his players eat steak and lobster."

We ended up winning the game by understanding the dream and committing to the dream during those hot summer practices.

You can never underestimate the importance of dreams.

I regret very few things. But I do have one regret at the University of Notre Dame where we took over a program that was down, and we went to the very top. You know what I regret? We stopped dreaming. We tried to maintain the place we were at. We should have set standards that people never thought were possible before. When you stop dreaming, you don't have enthusiasm. You just go through life and sort of let what happens happen.

What I'm talking about is not only for football. It's what I believe about life.

If you decide you want to go to a particular university, ask yourself twenty-five times a day, "What's important now?"

You have to have dreams—a purpose.

It's like the guy, John, who was on military guard duty.

He was dead tired after thirteen hours on his feet. He came back to the barracks and lay down on the bed. He couldn't move until he noticed a letter there from his dream girl.

He opened up the letter and it began "Dear John." Then it went on:

"If I could feel your strong, masculine arms embrace me, if I could gaze into those big, crystal blue eyes of yours one more time, if I could hear your sweet, tender voice just one more time, I know I could continue to be true. BUT. . . . "

All of a sudden John wasn't tired anymore.

He got up off that bed and went running off that military post doing about a 9.43 for the 100. The guard on duty saw him coming, took out his rifle, aimed it at John and yelled, "Halt."

John never broke stride.

The last words John uttered were these:

"My mother's in heaven. My father's in hell. My girl's in Chicago, and I'm going to see one of them tonight."

If you have that type of determination, you can't be stopped!

SELF-CONFIDENCE:

A SPECIAL PAGE IN THE PLAYBOOK

Did you know that you have 100,000 receptors in your eyes, 24,500 fibers in your ears, 200 bones, 500 muscles, and seven miles of nerve endings in your body?

Did you know that your heart beats 36 billion times a year and pumps the equivalent of 100,000 gallons of blood?

Did you know that every second two million of your blood cells die and are then replaced?

Did you know that your brain weighs three pounds and has 13 billion nerve cells?

None of this is an accident.

You are special.

And you can do special things.

Having self-confidence and a positive self-image is absolutely critical to being successful. But developing these is not so easily accomplished. We all experience other people putting us down. We all worry about not being accepted.

I was at the airport not long ago. A guy came up to me and said, "Anybody ever tell you that you look an awful lot like that Lou Holtz fellow, the football coach?"

"Oh yeah, it happens all the time," I joked.

He asked, "It kind of makes you mad, doesn't it?"

I just closed ranks and moved on. People put you down. It happens all the time.

After Notre Dame beat Southern California when we were ranked number one and they were ranked number two, our team went to Disneyland. I was asked to take a picture with our captains and Mickey Mouse and Donald Duck. I was then asked to pose for another photo. They put Pluto on my left and Goofy on my right. I thought it was a little weird, but I didn't say anything. I just pulled down my Notre Dame cap and smiled.

But then the picture ran in the *Los Angeles Times*. You can check it out. It ran the Monday after Thanksgiving, 1988. It's the one with Pluto, Goofy, and me. The caption said, "Here is Lou Holtz, head coach of the Fighting Irish of Notre Dame at Disneyland with Pluto and Goofy." Now that didn't bother me.

But then the next sentence was in bold capital letters. It stuck out at you. It said, "Lou Holtz is the one in the middle."

We all experience put-downs, good natured or otherwise. And they can affect our self-confidence. We have to develop a sense of humor about such things, move on, and not let them bother us.

People say dumb things all the time. Let me share two of my favorite all-time dumb quotes.

In 1899, the director of the U.S. Patent Office said, "We might as well close this office because everything that can be invented has already been invented."

In 1946, the president of Twentieth Century Fox said, "Television won't be able to hold on to any market it captures after the first six months because people will soon get tired of staring at a plywood box every night."

Now those are comments that were not on the mark at all. We know they are worth ignoring. The fact is people make comments that miss the mark all the time. Sometimes they are about us and we take them to heart. We mull them over and let them bring us down. They can become part of our self-talk. We say things like:

"I can't do this."

"Everyone's against me."

"I come from a poor home."

"My parents are divorced."

"No one in my family has ever gone to college, so I don't think I can either."

"I can never be fit because everybody in our family is overweight."

"No one is ever going to hire a teenager for a good job."

These statements rank with the ones above. We don't have to let anything hold us back. We can be as successful as we want to be.

How so? Now, that's not a stupid question at all.

In human relationships, people—including your parents, your teachers, your peers, your employers, and the person to your right and the person to your left—really only care about three things. They are best summed up in three questions people will ask you and you should ask yourself:

The first is, "Can I trust you?" The second is, "Are you committed to excellence?" and the third question is, "Do you care about me?"

When someone asks you, "Can I trust you?" what is going to be your response?

Without trust, no one really has a good chance for success.

It was obvious when I first came to coach football at the University of South Carolina that we did not have a great deal of trust on our team. I felt that was primarily because the players did not trust me. I had never had a problem like that before. Even after eighteen months on the job, I could tell the players still lacked trust. I just wasn't exactly sure where this lack of trust was rooted.

We had a team meeting at the end of June after a discipline problem arose. The players knew about the problem and hadn't told me. Had they trusted me enough, I could have resolved the problem before it became a national story. Now I wanted to know why they did not trust me enough to tell me what was going on.

At first, nobody said a word.

The longer their silence extended, the more frustrated I became.

Finally, one young man got up and spoke. "I do trust you, Coach. I think most of the players in this room trust you and the assistant coaches. But I don't trust many of my teammates in this room. Many of them lie."

He then proceeded to list a variety of other offenses his teammates had committed. When he sat down, some other players got up and expressed the same feelings that he had.

As a result of that team meeting we came up with a list of covenants, or agreements, that our football team would live by. For example, the players made an agreement that they were going to do things right, and that they would no longer sit by and watch one of their teammates do things that would jeopardize the team's chances for success.

I then passed out a blank sheet of paper to every member of the team. I asked them to write down all the things they did not like about themselves. After some time in silence, I told them to take those papers home and think about what they had written. In fourteen hours, we would meet again, and they would bring their papers with them.

When they returned, we gathered up all the papers without reading them. We took them to the practice field, put them in a pile, and burned them. We then dug a hole and buried the ashes. We put a blank tombstone over the spot.

I explained to our team that whatever they didn't like about themselves was now in the past. They were going to start a brand new life from that point on. All the mistrust and wrong decisions they had made in the past were over. And we now had agreements that we intended to live by.

I told them that the coaches and I would expect to see a different group of young men, a different group of students, a different team from that point on.

If you go out to the South Carolina practice field today, you will see a monument approximately three feet high with absolutely nothing marked on it. The reason we didn't mark anything on it is because the players alone know what's under there. They also know that the experience of burying their mistakes and dislikes of themselves changed their lives and changed their team.

Never underestimate how important it is to trust yourself and those close to you. And, if you do make a mistake, rectify it. Say you are sorry, bury the mistake, and move on with a positive attitude.

When you have a successful football team, I promise you, it's because the players trust the coach and the coach trusts the players. When you have a successful relationship, it's because those involved can trust one another. I've been able to be married for over forty years because my wife can trust me. And I can trust her. Trust is absolutely essential.

People say, "Well, how can I trust? How can I get people to trust me?"

Simple. Just do right.

Remember it is right to be honest, and it is right to be loyal.

If you just do what is right and avoid what is wrong, people will trust you. When they trust you, they respect you, and when they respect you, you will respect yourself.

It's also right to get over feeling guilty. There's not an individual alive, myself included, who hasn't done dumb things. We wish we hadn't done them. But you can't go through life with an albatross around your neck. All you need to do is say "I'm sorry" and make amends and move on. Happiness is nothing more than having a poor memory.

Don't be bitter. I think that's wrong. We all have had things happen to us that could make us bitter.

Maybe society has done you an injustice.

Or maybe you were hurt by a girlfriend or boyfriend.

Maybe a coach or a teacher.

Maybe you feel your parents have done you an injustice. Perhaps some of you have even experienced a parent walking out on you.

We all have reasons to be bitter. But resist the feeling. If you carry bitterness with you, it will make you negative.

You're going to complain about everything.

In the meantime, you're going to miss all kinds of opportunities because you have been focused on the wrong thing.

My wife was diagnosed with cancer several years ago. Subsequently the cancer spread to stage four in her throat. It was very serious, and she was very, very ill. But she never became bitter. She never became negative. Her positive attitude helped her to heal and overcome this life-threatening disease.

If you have a good image of yourself and have self-confidence, there isn't a problem in this world that you can't solve. And people will trust you if they believe that you will do what is right.

When you look at some of the problems experienced in schools you realize how little is understood about what is right and wrong. The Ten Commandments no longer hang on the walls in our public schools. The Supreme Court believed that put too much pressure on students to behave in a certain manner. Now we see more and more students who do not understand what is right.

In my coaching experience I've seen many talented athletes miss the opportunities their gifts provided them because they fouled up. They didn't do what is right.

If you really want to know how to get along with your fellow human beings, read and honor the book of Proverbs. On trust, Proverbs 3:5–6 says,

> **TRUST** *in the* **LORD** *with all your heart,*
> *on your own intelligence* **RELY NOT***;*
> *In all your ways be* **MINDFUL** *of him,*
> *and* **HE** *will make straight* **YOUR PATHS***.*

So always ask yourself, "Is this the right thing to do?"

Then, trust God to help you. Do what's right and avoid what's wrong. In that way, you will gain the trust of others.

The second question people will ask you is, "Are you committed to excellence?"

When you walk into a classroom the teacher wants to know, "Do you want to be good or are you just going through the motions?"

You can't pay people to excel. I was with Michael Jordan at the Jimmy Valvano Cancer Foundation Golf Tournament. As I sat there with Michael he pointed to an NBA All-Star player and said to me, "Lou, he will never win the championship."

The guy overheard us and said, "What do you mean? I've been all-pro."

Michael asked him, "How many pounds overweight are you?" The player said, "Thirty," but added, "We're not in camp right now."

And Michael replied, "That's why you won't win."

Michael Jordan's point was that if you want to be a champion you have to think about it, and you have to practice it—all the time, not just when somebody's looking or when somebody recognizes you.

As a coach I want athletes who are committed to excellence, not just because I'm around them, but because I can trust them to do the right thing because they know being committed to excellence is the right thing.

One of the differences between people to-day and a generation ago is that today people are concerned primarily about their rights and privileges.

A generation ago people were primarily concerned about obligations and respon-sibilities. They understood that when you joined a team, went to school, or took a job, obligations and responsibilities came along with them.

I believe one responsibility is that you have to want to be good. You have to want to be excellent.

And I can tell you from my experience that if an individual is going to be successful in one area, he or she can do well in every other area of his or her life.

We have all heard of the fine athlete who is a very poor student. Some people may say that is because the person has much more natural talent in athletics than in academics. There is certainly some truth to this.

But it is also a fact that a top athlete can take the same commitment to excellence that helped him or her to reach that level and ap-ply it to the classroom as well. And they will do better in the classroom.

I have found that most of the players I have coached who were very good in college and went on to professional careers did everything they could to make themselves not only outstanding on the playing fields, but also outstanding in the classroom.

This is one reason why our team grade point average at the University of South Carolina went from a 2.03 when I first arrived to almost a 2.7 within the first two years. And this happened as the students were moving ahead into upper division courses which were more difficult. Their feeling of pride in doing everything to the best of their ability carried over from the football field to the classroom.

The last question people will ask you is, "Do you care about me?"

You'll never find a person who doesn't need any encouragement.

You'll never find a person who doesn't need you to share a smile.

This is because everybody you meet has a problem. This includes your teachers, your principal, and your parents.

They may have a sick child, a sick in-law, a sick wife.

They may have financial problems.

They may have a relative getting ready to go to jail.

You don't know.

Let me tell you how our football team learned this lesson.

Most colleges and universities, including the ones I've coached, have an intra-squad game to end our spring practice. Years ago we would reward the winning team with a post-game steak dinner. The losers had to eat hot dogs and beans. We discontinued this when I found out that most of the players would rather eat hot dogs, hamburgers, and baked beans than steaks.

So we chose another way to reward the "losers" for their inability to succeed in the spring game. Over the years, we have had those players do things like donate blood to the American Red Cross, sponsor a charity car wash, and clean up litter on the highway. The list of such activities really goes on and on.

What has impressed me most is what seems to have followed from that, and that is the community service our football teams have done on their own. Our players obviously come from good, solid families who have given them outstanding training. There is not a week that goes by that I do not receive a letter from someone in the community, or from a school, or a charitable organization, commending several of our players for their service. In these cases, the players do this without any fanfare. I can assure you that nobody on our staff knew that they were involved in these particular endeavors. They did it on their own.

I think most teenagers realize that there have been some very special people in their lives who have helped them immeasurably. You may not have realized how much these special people cared for you at the time, but now you only wish you could say "thanks" and repay them. Sometimes you may think that it is not possible.

Let me tell you, you can repay them. You can repay those people who did so many outstanding things for you and helped you to accomplish so much by passing their care on to another person. You can show the same care they had for you to someone else.

When you "pass it on" in this way, don't expect anything in return—any compensation, publicity, or praise. Just do it because of your obligation to help other people as you have been helped in the past.

The need is there. I don't care if it's the President of the United States. I don't care if it's the class valedictorian, the star quarterback, or the homecoming queen. Everybody you meet is going to need some encouragement, some care.

I remember when I was in grade school. Our family did not have an abundance of money. My mom would buy me one pair of overalls and one shirt, and I would have to wear them the entire school year. She would wash them on the weekends. Then I would put them on again on Monday and start all over.

For a couple of years, nobody noticed I only had one set of clothes. But during my freshman year in high school my dad spilled some paint on my shirt that didn't wash out. So naturally I had a speckled shirt and everybody could tell I wore it day after day.

People made fun of me.

People laughed at me.

Some even bullied me.

I was not the only person in high school who was the butt of jokes, innuendoes, and cynical remarks. Being bullied at school is certainly not new.

But how well you handle such situations can help determine how well you are going to be able to handle this type of adversity the rest of your life.

When I was in high school some of these problems resulted in fistfights here and there. But with my height, weight, and size, I learned to rely on my wit and sense of humor to solve a problem. I came from an area where hunting was very popular, so many of my classmates had access to guns. But no one ever thought of using a gun to solve a school problem.

I believe we should never pass judgment on people because of the way they look, dress, wear their hair, or for their religious or political beliefs. For that matter, to get to know another person, you have to truly appreciate their background and their thoughts. When you have personal contact with someone, you do not look for ways he or she is different. You look at all the things you have in common. To get to know another person, you have to truly appreciate where they are coming from and how they see the world.

I feel that it is important for our football players to get to know each other better. Each night during two-a-day practices that are held before the season begins, I ask different players to get up and talk to the team about their backgrounds. It is unbelievable how the players come together when they understand what a person has gone through in his life. I can tell you that these meetings have moved me as deeply as they have the players.

At South Carolina, we average 82,000 fans per home game. This may not be impressive except that our stadium only seats 80,000. Many of these alumni and fans have written or told me that they have never seen a football team as close as the Gamecocks. This is because once the players had personal contact and understood each other better, they could find out how much they shared in common.

I was head football coach at Notre Dame for eleven years and spent many great afternoons in the stadium. But do you know what I remember most? The Special Olympics. In 1987, the University hosted the Special Olympics. Six thousand Special Olympians—people with handicaps and many reasons to be bitter and negative—competed in games for days. Yet all they want to do is love and be loved.

You know what I did? I was a hugger. I had lane three. My only job was to run up and hug whoever finished that race—first, last, or in between—in lane three. That and say, "I'm proud of you."

When I see people with talent, ability, and opportunity complain and get all upset because this person didn't talk to them or that person said something bad to them, I think of the Special Olympians and their loving, accepting attitudes.

on't forget, self-confidence and a good self-image is crucial for whatever you decide to be, whatever you decide to do, however you decide to be successful.

And keeping the implications of these questions in mind will help you significantly.

If you do what's right, it answers the question, "Can I trust you?"

When you always do everything to the best of your ability, it answers the question, "Are you committed to excellence?"

And when you encourage others, smile at them, speak with them, and don't make judgments about them based on appearances, it politely answers the question, "Do you care about me?"

Show your parents you care. Show your teachers. Show your fellow students. There is no such thing as magic in this area.

Think about someone you love and admire and respect. It could be a teacher. It could be a fellow student. I also want you to think about somebody you've got a problem with. Again, it could be anyone.

Now ask these three questions about both people. Answer with a simple "yes" or "no."

Can you trust them? Yes or no?

Are they committed to excellence? Yes or no?

Do they care about you? Yes or no?

I'll bet for the person you admire and re-spect you just said "yes" to all three questions. I also know with the person you've got a problem with, you've pinpointed the problem. Either you can't trust them, they're not committed, or they don't care.

One of my original 107 goals was to do magic tricks. And I've learned to do some. But there is absolutely nothing magical in how to get along with people. Like learning to do magic tricks, it takes effort to get along with others.

CONCLUSION

But thinking about the person I can't help but think about the dash. Because that represents a person's life and that will always last.

Let's review the Teen's Game Plan for Success just ever so briefly:

- Attitude is a choice you make. That's your choice.

- You're going to have to make sacrifices. Don't complain.

- Get rid of all the excuses for why you can't succeed.

- Always understand what you're trying to do.

- Finally, dream. Don't undersell yourself or your dreams.

I don't have much talent, and when I told you about my high school background, I was sincere. I was not a good athlete. But I have always been a dreamer. I hope you'll be a dreamer as well.

This game plan I've shared with you is something I really believe from the bottom of my heart. I hope you'll make it part of your life.

A FINAL POEM

A few years ago Notre Dame went over to Dublin, Ireland, to play the Naval Academy in football.

When we were over there, we went to a twelfth-century cemetery. All we saw was a group of dilapidated walls and huge tombstones.

One of our players, Alton Maiden, sat down at this cemetery and wrote a poem. I'd like to share this poem with you now.

THE DASH

I've seen death staring at me with
my own eyes in a way many
cannot know.
I've seen death take a lot of other
people and leave me here below.
I've heard many mothers' cries
but death refused to hear.
And in my life I've seen a lot of
faces filled with many, many
tears.

After death has come and gone a
tombstone sits for many to see.
It's not more than a symbol of a
person's memory.

I know the person's name.
I read the date of birth.
Dash.
And the date the person passed.
But the more I think about the
tombstone, the only important
thing is the dash.

Yes, I see the name of the person
but that I might forget.
I also read the date of birth and
death but even that might not
stick.
But thinking about the person I
can't help but think about the
dash.
Because that represents a person's
life and that will always last.

So when you begin to charter your
life make sure you're on a
positive path.
People may forget your birth and
death but always remember:
They'll never forget your dash.

—ALTON MAIDEN

AFTERWORD

BY LOU HOLTZ

When Ave Maria Press published *A Teen's Game Plan for Life* in 2002, I had no idea it would be as well received as it has been. The reason I can say this is because a day hardly passes that I don't receive a letter or comment about the positive effect this book has had on them as teenagers or as parents, grandparents, and coaches who work with teens.

Today, or thirty years from now, I couldn't add *one thing* to the lessons taught in this book that lead to a successful life. The ones taught on these pages have withstood the test of time. However, I would like teens to think about two more stories to help in forging a successful game plan for life.

Many times I have heard teenagers tell me they wish that their parents weren't such strong disciplinarians and would give them more freedom. In response, I would like them to consider the story of two young men who each received a puppy.

Both men loved their new puppies. However, the first owner just wanted his puppy to love him back so he allowed the puppy to do anything it wanted.

The first thing that the other young man did was to fit his puppy with a choke collar. Every time the puppy moved too far to the right or to the left, the choke collar pinched its neck. Many people told the man how mean and nasty he was to put a choke collar on the dog.

When the puppies were a year old, the second owner took off the choke collar and was able to walk through the neighborhood with his dog at his side. The dog enjoyed the neighbors, and everyone enjoyed the dog. The dog was free to sniff along the curbs and greet the children. The dog knew what it could and couldn't do. It had learned that freedom meant that there were parameters that would control actions. The dog loved the owner because he had helped the dog earn its freedom.

Meanwhile, the first owner who loved his dog but allowed it to do anything it wanted could never let his dog walk freely around the neighborhood or enjoy the neighbors and other dogs because it didn't know what conduct was acceptable or not. It hadn't learned the parameters of acceptable behavior when it was young.

So, I say to you, would you rather follow your parents' teachers', and coaches' rules of discipline so that you can enjoy a lifetime of responsible freedom? Or would you rather be allowed to do everything you want now and never fully learn how to be successful in the rest of your life? All successful people understand that rules and discipline help them achieve their success.

I know a very successful man by the name of Mitch Modell who owns approximately 150 sporting goods stores in the northeast called "Modell's." Mitch is a loving husband, devoted father, and one of the nicest men you will ever meet. I asked him one time about why he was so successful and he summed it up by saying "I want to make a difference."

Mitch went on to ask this question: "If I didn't go to work, who would miss me and why? If Modell's went out of business, why would it be missed?"

Mitch realized that because his stores' fair prices, quality merchandise, friendliness, and service were better than any of his competitors, people would miss them if they ever went away.

As long as you live the kind of life that people would miss you if you one day didn't show up, you are adding value to other people and ensuring success for your own life.

If you live by the three rules of this book:

1. Do right,
2. Do your best,
3. Show people you care,

then you will have success and you can be assured that you will be missed.

—June 2007

APPENDIX

COACH LOU HOLTZ

Lou Holtz, a college football analyst for ESPN and master motivational speaker, won 249 games (seventh best all-time) as a college football coach in a career spanning thirty-three seasons at six schools. Holtz is also the author of five books, including his recently released autobiography, *Wins, Losses, and Lessons* (HarperCollins, 2006).

Holtz was head football coach at the University of Notre Dame from 1986 to 1996, winning the National Championship in 1988. His teams were consistently ranked among the best in the nation.

In 2000, Holtz became the first coach to lead four different schools to top twenty finishes (North Carolina State, Arkansas, Notre Dame, and South Carolina).

Lou Holtz received a Bachelor of Science degree from Kent State University in 1959 and a Master of Arts degree in education from the University of Iowa in 1961. Coach Holtz and his wife Beth are parents to four grown children: Luanne, Skip, Kevin, and Elizabeth.

LOU HOLTZ'S
COLLEGIATE HEAD COACHING RECORD

School	Year	W	L	T	Pct.	Bowl/Opponent/Result/AP Rank
William & Mary	1969	3	7	0	.300	
William & Mary	1970	5	7	0	.417	Tangerine/Toledo/L 12-40
William & Mary	1971	5	6	0	.455	
N. Carolina St.	1972	8	3	1	.708	Peach/West Virginia/W 49-13/#17
N. Carolina St.	1973	9	3	0	.750	Liberty/Kansas/W 31-18/#16
N. Carolina St.	1974	9	2	1	.792	Bluebonnet/Houston/T 31-31/#11
N. Carolina St.	1975	7	4	1	.625	Peach/West Virginia/L 10-13
Arkansas	1977	11	1	0	.917	Orange/Oklahoma/W 31-6/#3
Arkansas	1978	9	2	1	.767	Fiesta/UCLA/T 10-10/#11
Arkansas	1979	10	2	0	.833	Sugar/Alabama/L 9-24/#8
Arkansas	1980	7	5	0	.583	Hall of Fame/Tulane/W 34-15
Arkansas	1981	8	4	0	.667	Gator/North Carolina/L 27-31
Arkansas	1982	9	2	1	.792	Bluebonnet/Florida/W 28-21/#9
Arkansas	1983	6	5	0	.545	
Minnesota	1984	4	7	0	.364	
Minnesota	1985	6	5	0	.545	Independence/Clemson/W 20-13

Notre Dame	1986	5	6	0	.455	
Notre Dame	1987	8	4	0	.667	Cotton/Texas A&M/L 10-35/#17
Notre Dame	1988	12	0	0	1.000	Fiesta/West Virginia/W 34-21/#1
Notre Dame	1989	12	1	0	.917	Orange/Colorado/W 21-6/#2
Notre Dame	1990	9	3	0	.759	Orange/Colorado/L 9-10/#6
Notre Dame	1991	10	3	0	.769	Sugar/Florida/W 39-28/#13
Notre Dame	1992	10	1	1	.864	Cotton/Texas A&M/W 28-3/#4
Notre Dame	1993	11	1	0	.900	Cotton/Texas A&M/W 24-21/#2
Notre Dame	1994	6	5	1	.542	Fiesta/Colorado/L 24-41
Notre Dame	1995	9	3	0	.750	Orange/Fla. St./L 26-31/#11
Notre Dame	1996	8	3	0	.727	#19
South Carolina	1999	0	11	0	.000	
South Carolina	2000	8	4	0	.667	Outback/Ohio St./W 24-7/#19
South Carolina	2001	9	3	0	.750	Outback/Ohio St./W 31-28/#13
South Carolina	2002	5	7	0	.417	
South Carolina	2003	5	7	0	.417	
South Carolina	2004	6	5	0	.545	

CAREER TOTALS

(33 seasons) 249-132-7 (.651) 12-8-2 (Bowl Games)

William & Mary (3 seasons) 13-20-0 (.394)

North Carolina State (4 seasons) 33-12-3 (.719)

Arkansas (7 seasons) 60-21-2 (.735)

Minnesota (2 seasons) 10-12-0 (.455)

Notre Dame (11 seasons) 100-30-2 (.765)

South Carolina (6 seasons) 33-37-0 (.493)